The Pre-Marital Assessment
For Couples That Are Looking To Unite
For A Long And Happy Marriage

WORKBOOK

First Edition

ISBN 13: 978-1494765866

Book Cover & Design by PIXEL eMarketing INC.

Legal Disclaimer

The Publisher and the Author make no representations or warranties with respect to the accuracy or completeness of the contents of this work and specifically disclaim all warranties, including without limitation warranties for a particular purpose. No warranty may be created or extended by sales or promotional materials. The advice and strategies contained herein may not be suitable for every situation.

Neither the publisher nor the author shall be liable for damages arising herefrom. The fact that an organization or website is referred to in this work as a citation and/or a potential source of further information does not mean that the author or the publisher endorses the information the organization or website it may provide or recommendations it may make.

Further, readers should be aware that Internet websites listed in this work may have changed or disappeared between when this work was written and when it is read.

To my Aunt and Uncle: Mary & John Borgen!

Your 72 years of marriage is a true reflection of what I believe is the ideal marriage.
Now in your 90s, your love for each other is still evident and inspiring.

Contents

Introduction

Just by showing up to take part in the *Eyes Wide Open Workbook,* you have already demonstrated a commitment to your own marriage. There is no true way for anything to completely prepare you for marriage, but a method like this is meant to get you thinking about the big picture. While there is no easy and quick fix to any marriage, it is always hopeful when two partners realize they need to invest the time and effort to make it work.

In fact, even a seemingly good marriage takes work in order to maintain that level of success. I know because I have also been there. After 20 years of marriage, I suffered through a long and painful divorce. This experience was the main motivation behind trying to understand why as many as 50% of marriages fall apart.

My hope is to help prevent more couples from enduring what my ex and I did. Tools like this *Eyes Wide Open Workbook* are intended to help, ultimately, in bringing that 50% down dramatically. Some of it is learning the basics of what so many people do not realize about making marriage work.

The number one misconception is that all you need is love to make a marriage work. This is not enough if you intend to have a long-term marriage. Maybe the motto for marriage should be "love is all you need_along with hard work." Yet anything you love requires work.

Whether it is your car, your home, or your children, they all require more than just love. To keep your car running, you need regular maintenance; in other words, work. To keep that dream home you designed yourself and fell in love with intact, it requires continuous hard work. From cleaning the gutters, to making small repairs, to having the roof replaced, it is the hard work that helps preserve what it is you love. Of course, with children, you can really see where you need more than love. From the moment that child enters the world, you can love it with all of your heart and more than you have ever loved anything else. That will not be enough though. It takes hard work to keep them safe, to help them grow into good people, and to prepare them to start a successful life on their own. Marriage is no different.

By reading the material I have provided and powering through this workbook, it shows that you are aware of that. Even if you did not realize before that marriage is about love and hard work, you probably see that now. By starting this new phase of your marriage, you are also showing devotion to making it work.

There are so many points in a marriage when this level of work is required. So it is important to realize this is an ongoing process. Use this workbook as many times as you need because life will continue to throw you challenges, and your marriage will continue to require hard work.

Newlyweds often find themselves feeling overwhelmed and even blindsided when those first big challenges start coming at them. That dreamy, idyllic honeymoon phase gives way to real life, which includes challenges such as:

- Career _ having your own and still having time for each other and sometimes even dealing with periods of unemployment
- Children _ deciding if you want any, how many, and then raising them
- Family holidays _ or get togethers
- Planning vacations _ or finding time to enjoy a vacation
- Buying a home and keeping it maintained
- Keeping your own identity as well
- Hobbies _ having some together and some of your own
- Finances _ keeping your household afloat, building a nest egg, and trying to see eye to eye on spending choices and habits
- Illness and Death _ dealing with illness and death in the family and supporting each other instead of letting it tear you apart

This is just a sample of those things in life that you do not think about having to address as a couple, usually until you are faced with it. Few people in the early dating period when you feel nothing but euphoria and early stages of marriage when the sex life is probably at its peak, think ahead to the future.

Tools like this workbook are meant to help prepare couples for the reality behind the scenes of the "happily ever after." If you are already married, it is meant to act as a life preserver before you both simply throw in the towel. Either way, it should hopefully serve to wake you up to the fact that no marriage is perfect but the perfect couple will be ready, willing, and eager to still travel down that road together.

This is not a crash course. Take your time in working through the *Eyes Wide Open Workbook*. Some of the questions are easier, and some require more thought and possibly even some soul searching. Rushing through this will only be a disservice to you, your partner, and your marriage as a whole.

Some of what is included is meant to be done individually, and some is for the couple together. This is already much like the steps through marriage. Make sure you allot enough quiet time to focus on the questions and the work. Do not do it half-heartedly as though it is chore like doing the laundry.

This is your marriage at stake here. The work you invest will only serve you better in the long run. You should also be honest about what you discover along the way. You may uncover things you did not know or already see challenges presenting themselves.

This is the perfect time to get these out in the open and begin working through them. Yes, there is even a chance this workbook could be an eye opener and game changer in which you realize you may not be as compatible as you had hoped. In cases like this, you should, at the very least, give yourself some more time as a couple before jumping into a marriage.

The main purpose is to give you what you need to build a strong marriage. But with the initial understanding, hard work is as important as love when it comes to building a healthy marriage.

1

The Love Connection

In any loving relationship that leads to marriage, there are things you need to consider and questions that should be asked, discussed, and reflected upon:

Are both of you emotionally available?

No. Bwahahahahaha. DEAD

Will you be able to seek personal fulfillment when you are with your spouse?

Yes.

For sure 75% of my personal fulfillment comes from seeing Aiem Happy

Do you have a server's heart _ something required from both a man and woman in a happy marriage?

Maybe. "Sometimes."

I like to think I have a servers attitude more often than not.

Do you practice gratitude? How thankful are you for your life with the person you intend to marry?

Yes.

Maybe not enough?
Maybe not in the right way.

Can you surrender and put someone else before yourself when it matters?

Yes

Yes

Do you keep a thanksgiving journal to remind you of the good things in your relationship?

Starting it - really?

I dont have a specific journal, but I do intentionally keep momentos around to remind us of good times.

Now consider these tough questions about love:

What is truly important in your significant other?

Understanding & Communication

Thats a good answer because it can be applied in so many ways. So lets go with that.

What do you really want in a potential spouse?

beautiful
Smarter than me
Knows value of work
fun yet predictable

Deep down, who is the person you are thinking of marrying?

Archi. Everyday is an adventure with her.
I want to make her happy everyday.

Are you emotionally, mentally, and spiritually prepared to take this step in life?

haha damn, I'm doubting myself now
because of the way that q is asked.

Is this person your best friend, or could they become your best friend?

I think so, but you'd have to ask her. Especially since we started dating bc I "didn't want to be her friend."

Do you thoroughly enjoy being with each other?

LOL. I can't.

Do you have common interests and things you like to do together?

Yeah, and I'm always open to new things ~~that~~ besides marathons.

Do you have things you like to do on your own?

Remember, love gives you the level of commitment you need to invite someone else to share your life with you. If you do not think that is hard, think of how difficult it has been to spend your life alone until now.

2

Aligning Beliefs and Values

When it comes to beliefs and values, it is important to understand where your significant other stands. At their core, these differences can result in more problems than they are worth in a marriage that has not been carefully considered.

Define your personal beliefs and values about:

1) Life is about relationships.

(1) child • respect
sibling/friend • support
lover/parent • complete dedication & attentiveness

(2) schools
teams
work
body
etc

2) Love

What should marriage be?

a partnership that is mutually beneficial and honest and FUN!!!

What is your ideal version of marriage?

LOL. Aichi stays sexy & sassy forever.

What do you value in a partner for life?

intelligence. logic. dedication.
communication. Fairness & tact.
patience, perspective & predictability

Define what you understand to be the beliefs and values of your future spouse.

Family
Honesty
Integrity
Money
Power
Love
Beauty

What do you believe or have faith in? Does your partner feel the same way?

I believe in love

Do you trust your future spouse?

Hell yes

Common Beliefs and Values Assessment

Write out the following list of words, ranking them in importance. Each partner should write down their feelings about the word to expose their core beliefs. Then swap and discuss.

Example: *Honesty: Very important, but white lies are all right to spare someone's feelings*

- Honesty

- Commitment

- Loyalty

- Fidelity

- Kindness

- Self-control

- Education

- Parental Devotion

- Children

- Friendship

- Sacrifice

- Living Simply

- Peace Making

- Generosity

- Love

You can add or remove words in this list to see if the two of you share similar core values and beliefs. Of all the factors in marriage that matter, this is one of the big ones. Constant fighting and arguments are hard to overcome when your values are not aligned.

3

Marriage Expectations

During my research, I discovered that not only is addressing marriage expectations rare, but it comes as a surprise to couples that have been together for a long time. Why do we spend weeks choosing which car to buy but fail to do the same with our potential life partners?

Before you get married, answer these questions. It will make the transition into married life a heck of a lot easier!

What do you expect of your future husband / wife?

To love me in good times and in bad.

What dominant role in the household will you play?

I'll get all the stuff done on top of doing what I do, so that as much time as possible is available for Archi to enjoy instead of neurotically try to take care of stuff.

Archi will work and love me.

What dominant role in the household will your spouse play?

What chores will you take on?

Long list for CPO	Archi
	Be reasonable

What chores will your spouse take on?

Who will primarily raise the kids?

Conversation: I assume I would do like 95% so anything you want is available to you...

How much time should be spent together?

Lots, but not too much.

How much time should be spent apart?

just enough

Who handles the financial management concerns?

What needs are most important for you to meet?

I don't know.

What needs are most important for your spouse to meet?

Describe your ideal marriage.

Two happy people who make each other better and enjoy life together.

Describe a nightmare marriage.

Yelling & Screaming
refusal to compromise
lack of understanding/fairness towards each other.

Once you have answered these core expectation questions, you will have a clear path forward. Sit together and discuss it all. Do not leave anything out. Laugh about your unrealistic expectations, and carefully consider your realistic ones.

New expectations will arise all the time at crucial turning points in a good marriage, so keep an eye out for them. If you need to, revisit this conversation again and again as your perceptions change. Becoming parents, buying your first home, dealing with illness_you will have to learn to accommodate each other's expectations in order to be happy.

4

Career Matching

My advice would be to sit down with your fiancé or potential fiancé and have a good long chat about your career aspirations. Do not be afraid to add in your dreams to the very height of their potential. Be bold, and be honest.

Men _ What do you want? Do you want a career-minded woman or a woman that is happy to stay at home with the kids? Explore your feelings.

Career minded woman who can make up for contributions women didn't get to give for too long

Women _ What do you want? A career-driven man that makes a lot of money but places heavy work demands on his time, a man that has a balanced career, or a man that will not mind staying at home with the kids?

What are your career goals? Start from now, and trace a direct line of progression to the very top of your career _your ideal position.

Will both partners work? If you do, who will look after the kids?

Who will be responsible for the kids during the day?

Will there be travel requirements, and how will they affect the family unit?

What is your tolerance to risk? If you marry an entrepreneurial spirit, they cause severe financial fluctuations that do not fit in with the traditional "stable" household.

Would you be willing to marry someone that aims to be an entrepreneur?

Do you prefer a partner that is more secure _ with a stable job?

How will career transfers be handled? Would you be willing to move to another state to advance your partner's career?

____

____

____

____

____

____

How many of the above questions did you answer that were based on the idea of gaining financial reward? Is this important to you?

Consider these questions carefully with your partner so that you can clearly align your career goals for a healthier, happier marriage.

Your Roles in Marriage

When you are discussing your ideal marriage roles, you will encounter points of disagreement that need to be worked on. Put those aside until the end. Then find a fair compromise and work through it together.

What is a man's role in a marriage?

What is a women's role in a marriage?

Who will do the cooking?

Who will do the cleaning?

Where will the income of the household come from?

Is equality in everything important to you?

As a man, are you willing to take a more active role with the kids?

As a woman, are you willing to take a more active role with money?

What makes you happiest _ working or being with the kids?

Where do your expectations come from?

What is expected of each partner on certain holidays?

Who is going to do all the shopping?

Who is going to take out the trash?

Who is responsible for initiating sex?

____

____

____

____

____

____

Keep in mind that very few people are "right" about their roles in marriage. What is right for you, may not be right for your partner. There will be a certain amount of compromise required from you both, but hey _ you would be doing it alone anyway if you were single, right!

Do not think of living with your partner as living with your previous family members. Your wife is not your mother; she will not enjoy hearing complaints about how she has not cleaned up YOUR mess. A good marriage takes two people _ two very realistic people.

6

Responsibilities in Marriage

When you take a jaunt into the volatile world of responsibility division, expect some difficult choices and tough negotiations. You both need to be happy with the division of labor. If you want to keep it fresh, switch chores.

I do not know how you are going to do it, but you will know when it works. There will be less fighting, and things will get done. Both of you have to pull your weight. Personal and domestic responsibility is a must-have in a happy marriage.

Is your partner capable of comfortably accomplishing the chores they need to do on their own?

Does your future spouse need or want help with most chores?

Do you both feel better completing tasks as a team?

Are you willing to jump in and assist when your partner needs you to?

Where do you think resentment could arise?

When do each of you struggle to achieve your daily chores?

What can you do to lighten the load?

Can you afford to hire some help for the chores that neither of you want to do?

How can you make chore-time special as a couple?

I found that resentment is often involved with chores when one individual feels like they are doing all of the work. Interestingly, when a couple does a horrible chore together, it can do the opposite, which benefits and strengthens their marriage.

Responsibility is about the division of labor and accountability. But it is also about helping your spouse when they need it, asking for help when you need it, and keeping those lines of communication open.

Communication Wars

Communication is really the foundation of any happy marriage. You can only build on a quality foundation! That is why for a new couple that is considering marriage, you must answer the following questions:

How do you communicate with people?

____

____

____

____

____

____

How well do the two of you listen to each other?

Do you listen and affirm with your eyes and body language?

Is your partner quiet and calm in most situations?

Is your partner combative, emotional, and a screamer in most situations?

Do you share your feelings on a daily basis with your partner?

Do you share how you need to be communicated with?

When do you feel most connected with your partner?

Have you developed any positive signals or gestures to aid in communication?

Do you have negative signals or gestures that need to be cast away?

Frankly, marrying a person that cannot or will not communicate with you effectively is a massive mistake. The only chance that the two of you have to enjoy a happy marriage together is to be able to speak to each other in a way that you cannot do with anyone else.

The whole point of having a partner is to share your life with them. Yet we forget to do that every day through effective communication. Let them in, and be a part of their lives in every way possible _ and you will be happy together.

Decision Making Abilities

Decision making in married couples needs to be firmly united but also brimming with wisdom. That is the only way that you will be able to move forward happily. This is why choosing the right marriage partner is so important.

Who is your "go to" person for advice, counsel, and wisdom?

____

____

____

____

____

____

Who do you seek spiritual advice from?

Who do you seek personal advice from?

Who do you seek relationship advice from?

Who do you seek business advice from?

Who do you seek financial advice from?

Does your future partner have the ability to offer advice in these areas?

Who will the people be that both of you as a couple seek wisdom from?

Are the decisions from the person that you plan on marrying well thought out, or are they impulsive?

Are the long-term ramifications for your spouse's decisions thought out?

In your opinion, what is the best decision that you have ever made?

What was the worst decision that you have ever made?

When you disagree during the decision making process, do you express it?

What will you both make decisions about once you are married?

Who will have the final decision if a consensus cannot be reached?

Work through these questions with your future partner and compare notes. You will be surprised what you find! Have the maturity to chat through it and come to your first unified decision.

9

Family History Lessons

A genogram is a family diagram, which can be thought of as an elaboration of the family tree. Genograms contain a wealth of information on the families represented because they allow you to illustrate not only how members of a family tree relate to each other, but how they are a product of their time, by their behaviors, friendships, and many more.

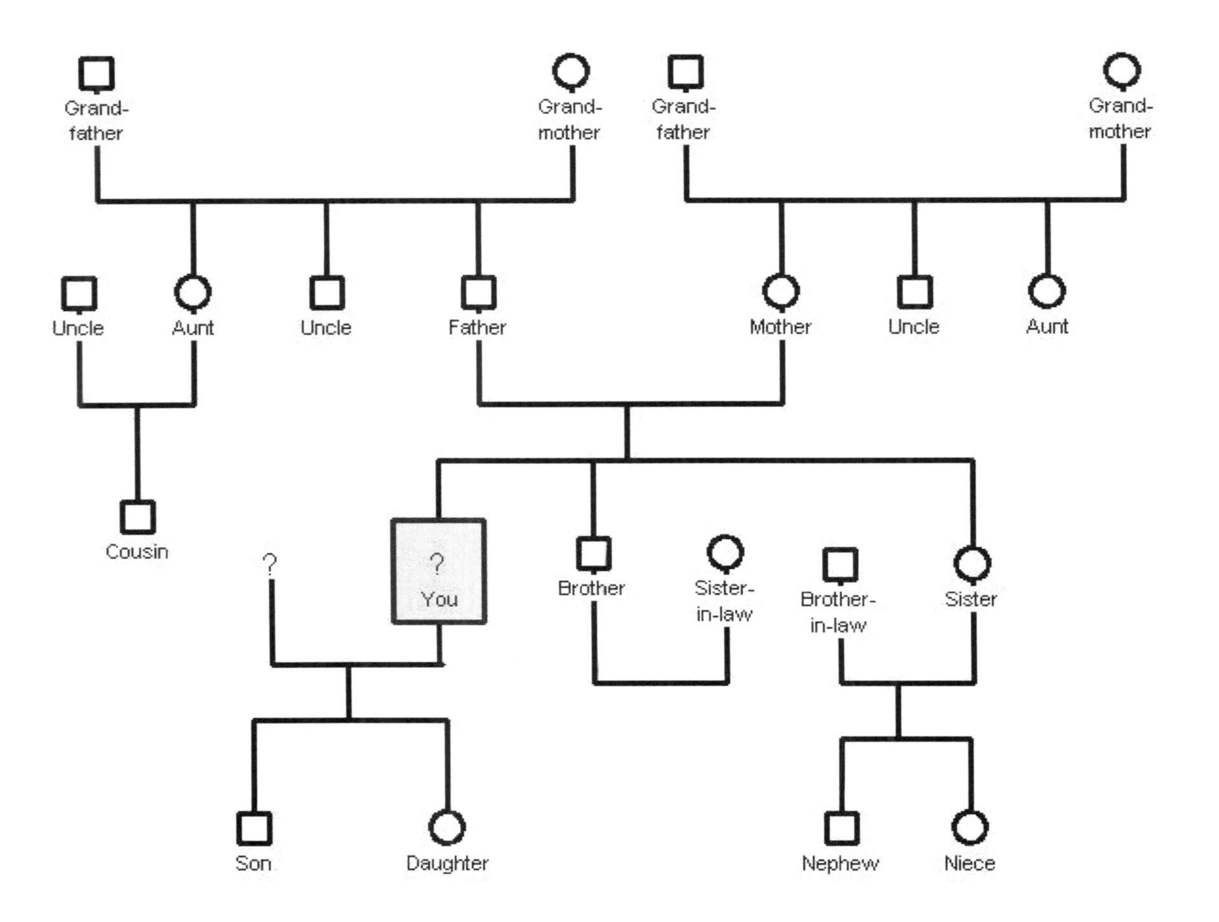
Grand-
father
Grand-
mother
Grand-
father
Grand-
mother
Uncle
Aunt
Uncle
Father
Mother
Uncle
Aunt
Cousin
?
?
You
Brother
Sister-
in-law
Brother-
in-law
Sister
Son
Daughter
Nephew
Niece

Create your Genogram here:

When drawing up your very own genograms, there are some questions that you will need to answer. Here is what you need to know:

Are there conflicts between family members? Watch out for patterns where issues are not resolved in your family.

Is anyone cut off or alienated? People that stop talking to each other have poor communication skills.

Are there any distant or poor emotional connections in your family?

Is there pressure for family members to think, feel, or act alike? Sometimes there can be a low tolerance for members that are separate or different.

Is there any form of abuse? Sexual, emotional, physical, or otherwise?

Briefly discuss your generational patterns and how each family relates to the other. Include things like addictions, affairs, bad relationship choices, abuse, divorce, mental illness, depression, family secrets, out of wedlock births, health issues, unemployment, and poor financial decisions.

Once you have done that, write down any huge events that sent shockwaves through the family: pre-mature death, abandonment, suicide, war, cancer, personal financial destruction, business collapse, or affairs. Get everything out on the table!

How have these relational patterns and events affected who you are?

How have you dealt with these issues?

Are they affecting you today?

Do any of these patterns currently affect how you make decisions?

Can you deeply understand that your future spouse may respond in certain ways that may make you feel uncomfortable when a hot button issue is touched?

When you understand what is below the surface in the heart of your potential partner and proceed to discuss the issues, be gentle_there may be residual feelings there. Your job is to guard your heart and be sensitive to your partner's feelings as well.

Working With Fears

When it comes to fear, it is essential that you get it all out for each other to see. People very rarely discuss what they are afraid of; least of all with the people they love. But discussion leads to understanding, which in turn refocuses your relationship on support and love.

Before you make the decision to get married, run through these questions on fear with your intended. Together, find some time to discuss them.

What are you most afraid of?

What is your future spouse most afraid of?

Are your fears justified, or are they imagined?

What can you do to overcome your fears?

How can you reassure your partner when their fears surface?

When do your fears crop up the most?

What are the warning signs that fear is overwhelming you?

Focus on these questions for a few hours one evening. There is nothing more proactive than allowing your future spouse to see your vulnerabilities. If you are committed to this marriage, then you should have no problem exploring all of your fears with your loved one.

Take note of the warning signs, and put a plan in place to recognize and deal with your fear when it does crop up in your marriage. For now, identification and assessment are as close as you are going to get, but when your fear hits again, new insights will be uncovered.

If your partner does not want to talk about their fears with you, they are not committed to your successful marriage. If they do not want to put in the work now, they will not do it later. Then fear may be the reason that your relationship falls to pieces.

Hurts and Losses 101

There are several questions that you should think about discussing with your potential spouse before getting married. Discussing these issues will give you insight into the way that you and your intended deal with emotional distress.

Have you grieved your losses?

What kinds of wounds has your partner suffered?

Do they still carry around emotional pain from these experiences?

Are you being seen as the answer to their pain?

Have you ever successfully consoled your partner when they are upset?

____

____

____

____

____

____

How is the best way to go about consoling your partner?

____

____

____

____

____

____

Each one of us has developed a unique coping style when we have to deal with painful emotional experiences. There are many methods of recovery that you can use to help each other get over a significant emotional blow:

- Talk to family and friends
- Seek counseling
- Engage in social activities
- Exercise often

- Eat health food
- Seek spiritual support
- Take time to relax
- Join a support group
- Listen to good music
- Be patient with yourself
- Know that feeling grief is okay
- Keep and write in a journal
- Make a serious effort to serve someone less fortunate than yourself

Dealing with loss and hurt is a part of our daily lives. Sometimes it can be something small, like the loss of a project at work. Other times it can be something huge, like the loss of a close friend. Whatever happens, it happens to both of you, together.

You can either choose to respond negatively to it and compound the emotional distress or you can respond positively and reduce their distress considerably. There are only these two choices, so make sure that you both know that.

Open Signs of Concern

We all have areas of concern that we have to work on. Nobody is perfect! But there is a big difference between someone that is willing to work through their issues and someone that will not even admit to having them.

For an easier marriage experience, your future partner must be committed to hearing your opinions and offering their own in your life. Share, be honest, and do not hide things from each other. It is extremely unhealthy!

Based on this chapter's list, are you concerned about anything?

____

____

____

____

____

____

What does alcohol do to your potential spouse?

Does your potential spouse flirt with other people when you are around?

Does the majority of your conversation revolve around them?

Are you given the loving respect you deserve?

Do they value your opinions?

Is the person you are with trustworthy?

Does your partner care for themselves and their home?

What are their habits when purchasing and spending?

Is their life balanced with various activities and pursuits?

Does your future spouse give you the attention that you need?

Do they make you feel safe and allow for vulnerability?

Is your guard up around your future spouse?

Can you be honest with your partner?

____

____

____

____

____

____

These questions will help you both expose the areas of concern that may affect your marriage in the future. If there are issues here to address, do them before the wedding. Otherwise, some years later, you may find yourself wondering why you just "left it."

Stress, Stress, and More Stress!

A married couple that sticks together through stressful times grows closer together. But you must be aware of the challenges that you will face if you or your partner are very stressed all the time and do nothing about it.

That is why you must assess your own stress levels and the stress levels that your partner has. If you find that you are bickering often, do some activities together that promote healthy stress relief. Do not, and I mean do not, ignore the problem!

Based on the list of ailments, are you handling stress well?

Is your partner handling stress well?

Are you seeing healthy and unhealthy patterns dealing with your stress levels?

Is the choice to go for a good strenuous workout or sit back with a few cold beers?

Do you drink wine every day after work?

Are there periods in your life of excessive drama?

How do you usually deal with stress?

Now that you know how, will you work on stress as a couple?

____

____

____

____

____

____

A married couple is a strong, united force when both people are aligned and working towards their common happiness. Unfortunately, when both people are stressed, the opposite happens.

You would never believe how many more problems can result from stress co-existing with you in your marriage. If both of you are highly stressful people, you may want to consider the implications of that. It would be far better for a neurotic person to marry a relaxed personality. While this cannot always happen, something must be done about your stress.

Dealing With Adversity

Adversity is coming, and you need to be prepared for it. That is why you need to know how your partner responds to challenges in their own lives. Spend an evening asking each other these valuable questions.

Make sure that you answer honestly and that at the end you both make a commitment to face these obstacles together as a team. Together you are strong, but there is no stress, pain, and loneliness like a marriage where only one person deals with adversity.

Does your future spouse know what adversities you have faced in your life?

Do you know what your future spouse has faced in their life?

How have you and your spouse overcome your challenges?

How have you been affected by them?

What did you or your spouse learn from these challenges?

What kind of growth has come out of it?

What adversity can both of you anticipate during your marriage?

How will you deal with those hardships?

____

____

____

____

____

____

Keep in mind that balance in a healthy marriage is very important. While there will always be one dominant partner in the marriage, the other should not be allowed to shirk responsibility so that one individual has to face these problems alone.

If your future spouse does not have a great track record with adversity, then you either need to get them to face their problems or they will not be around to help you face yours — even if it concerns both of you. That is the lesson that adversity teaches us.

Children Matter

Children can be an eternal source of joy, but they can also be a living nightmare if you have not discussed how you feel about having kids with your future spouse. Telling your spouse four years into your marriage that you do not want children is unfair to both of you.

The same goes for having kids, despite the fact that you never really wanted them in the first place. This is not an acceptable level of commitment for such a huge decision. Talk about it now by answering the following questions:

Do both of you want children?

How many children do each of you want?

How many siblings do you have?

How do you envision your life with your children?

How to you see your life without children?

How will both of you make time for your marriage with the responsibility of kids running around the house?

Who will get up in the early hours of the morning when the child is sick?

If one spouse is infertile, how will it be handled?

Will you have no children, will you adopt, or will you use a surrogate?

If no kids are your only option because you or your spouse are infertile, can your marriage survive that kind of emotional trauma?

Once you have addressed these questions, you should gain a better understanding of what sort of life you are going to have with your future spouse. If you always dreamed of kids but your spouse refuses to have any, it will cause problems and lead to divorce.

16

Parenting Problems

Becoming a parent is one of the most exciting experiences anyone can go through. With the right spouse, it can be a magical journey and a new stage in your life. But parenting is not for everyone, and you have to make sure that your ideals align with your future spouse's.

If you both disagree on how to raise your kids, there will be endless fighting. Sometimes this can cause so much trouble in a marriage that it ends. To avoid this outcome, evaluate the true feelings that your partner has on parenting and how they aim to do it one day.

How was each one of you parented?

____

____

____

____

____

____

Were your parents warm, loving, and affectionate?

____

____

____

____

____

____

Were they cool, distant, and critical?

____

____

____

____

____

____

Did your parents hover over you with little room to breathe?

Were you allowed to make decisions and learn from your choices _good or bad?

Was your home life very structured, or did your parents "wing it"?

Was perfection something that you were expected to achieve?

How were you disciplined? Did you get time outs, spanking, or more chores?

Did your parents set expectations for you?

Did you live in a high tension home, or was it relaxed?

Did you have assigned chores to do on a weekly basis?

Were your academic achievements important?

Were there any issues relating to teen alcohol or drug use?

How were problems handled when you were a child?

Were there any traumatic events in the family that affected the children?

When you have both answered all of these questions and discussed it thoroughly, you will find that you understand why you want to parent in a particular way. Most parenting styles are based on what was learned from childhood or what was not enjoyed in childhood.

Fighting Styles

Once you properly understand how each of you fights, you will be able to defuse situations before they arise_which is key to having a successful marriage. There are many crucial questions that you should address, which will shed some light on your "couple's fighting style" as you move forward together.

Ask each other these questions, and discuss them in detail.

Have the two of you had a disagreement or fight before?

How did your parents used to fight, and do you fall into the same patterns?

Looking back, what did you observe about each other's fighting style?

How long do your fights last?

Was it destructive warfare like trying to rip each other's hearts out or scratch at each other's eyes?

Was anything said that was truly hurtful that you regretted later on?

Was anything brought up from the past?

Did one party keep quiet during the heated situation?

Did anyone walk out or leave?

Was there any form of revenge taking?

Was it constructive fighting?

Did both of you remain calm and try to understand each other then find a solution to the issue?

Was there direct and careful communication?

Did the issue get resolved?

What agreements were made going forward?

How can both of you work toward resolving conflict constructively in future?

If you fight like cats and dogs or have unhealthy ways of fighting with your future spouse, you will want to sort that out before getting married. Marriage is not about who wins in these fights but how you can resolve them so that peace and love return to the household.

18

Money Woes and Wins

Money is an essential part of life, and we all need to be cautious of it in a marriage to someone new. Understanding how your future spouse operates with your finances will allow you to either teach them or assist them in learning how to properly manage money.

It is so easy for one partner in a marriage to bring the household to its knees by overspending. Know how each of you functions with money, make a plan, and avoid falling into the debt trap that ruins so many young couples from the start.

Ask each other these questions.

Is the person you are marrying a good steward of finances?

Do both of you have a budget that you have constructed together to move forward with a financial plan for the future?

What does he or she spend money on?

What is important to each of you? Car, clothes, dining out, toys, travel?

____

____

____

____

____

____

Do you ever find yourself purchasing to impress or keep up with other people?

____

____

____

____

____

____

Do you give to a charity or 10% of your income to your church?

____

____

____

____

____

____

Do you use a credit card or a debit card?

Do you know what his or her credit score is?

Are you able to get on the same page financially with your future spouse?

Does your future spouse spend without consideration, or do they wait for sales?

What financial blemishes do you have from the past that may affect your future? Bankruptcy? Heavy credit card debt?

What did you learn from these tough financial times?

Are you prepared for your future? Job loss? Sickness? Retirement? College funds?

Is it possible to put away 10% of both of your incomes or more?

If you are in agreement to have children, what will you teach them about money?

Are you debt averse?

When it comes to investment, are you risk or security orientated?

Get through these questions and orientate yourself in how much each of you understands about money. If you do not know much, start learning now.

19

Needs, Wants, and Desires

Needs, wants, and desires may feel secondary to everything else, but they keep you whole, and they drive you forward in a good marriage. That is why you have to know how your future spouse functions and what their needs truly are. Fulfilling them or helping them become fulfilled is part of your job as a spouse.

Answer these questions together and discuss the results:

Do you feel safe expressing your needs, wants, and desires to your potential spouse?

Do you feel appreciated for your loving acts of kindness?

Is your partner supporting your dreams, goals, and pursuits?

Do you allow time alone for each of you when you really need it?

Do you believe in each other's talents?

Are you both acknowledging and affirming each other?

Do you say "I love you" at least once a day?

Are you playing together?

Are you letting your partner live out their adventure?

Are you encouraging them to be dangerous?

Do you feel that this person will protect you / have your back?

Do you feel listened to and understood by your partner?

Do you respect each other?

How do you know that you truly know your partner's heart?

Do you listen instead of trying to fix each other all the time?

Do either one of you talk about yourself continuously?

How did your parents relate when it came to expressing needs, wants, and desires?

In observing your partner, do they express what their needs are?

Do you have an agreement that you will help each other around the home?

How will you handle and divide responsibilities with the kids?

When you take the time to answer these questions, you will get to know how each of you feels about these important elements in your relationship. Needs, wants, and desires drive us, so knowing your partner's is a great start.

20

Love Making and Sex

Even though sex in marriage is almost the same as sex outside of marriage, there are still some important questions to address before either of you take the leap into married life. Promise to both answer these questions honestly and directly, so that things do not surface later on in your marriage to cause dissention.

Do you have any sexually transmitted diseases?

How many sexual partners have you had in your lifetime?

Have I ever hurt you in the way I have treated sex in the relationship and how?

Do you ever struggle with sexual impulses or temptation?

After sex, how do you feel about the relationship?

What do you really like during foreplay?

Is there anything specific you would like to try in the bedroom?

What does it mean to you when I climax?

What do I do during sex that you really enjoy?

Do you think we are sexually compatible?

Do you think that we set a good sexual foundation for the kids?

What can each of you do to improve the sexual intimacy in your relationship?

How can you show your partner that you are sexually attracted to them?

Being sexually connected in marriage is key to drawing closer together as a couple. By exploring your feelings about sex with each other, you can arrive at a wealth of knowledge that will help you improve how you relate to one another in the bedroom.

This is instrumental to a newly married couple that wants to make sure that their sex lives are well-rounded and healthy. Explore these questions and get the answers you need.

21

God and Religion

In a Christian marriage God comes first, then the man, then the woman. But both of the individuals in the married couple are under God and are expected to adhere to certain religious conventions.

Similar conventions are true of other religions. Some couples are more religious than others, but it is important to know where each of you stands before the big decisions are made.

If you want to find out how spiritual your future spouse is, ask these questions:

Are you a spiritual person?

What do you believe in?

Do you attend religious services regularly and how often?

What is your understanding of a Godly marriage?

How will faith impact your marriage?

What do you expect from your future spouse, religiously speaking?

What is the role of the wife in *[insert religion]* marriage?

What is the role of the husband in *[insert religion]* marriage?

What is your relationship like with the church, synagogue, temple, etc.?

Do you volunteer to serve in your community through your house of worship?

What is the relationship like between you as a couple, and the other couples of faith in your area?

Are you prepared to raise kids as [insert religion] in your household?

Once you have answered these questions you will be able to gauge whether or not your future spouse has the same beliefs as you, and if they are going to support your faith through your marriage. Couples that pray together, stay together after all. It sounds cliché, but being united in faith is one of the finest parts of marriage.

Closing Words

My honest and genuine hope for you now is that you are ready to take on whatever life has to bring you, the good and the bad, as a couple. There is no way to ever be fully prepared for the highs and lows life is full of. There is also no way to guarantee a 100% happy, healthy marriage now and until death do you part.

Yet you can increase your likelihood for success. You should also have a better and more realistic idea of what goes into a marriage. Most importantly, you should, by now, have been awakened to the fact that marriage is not based on just love.

Hopefully you realize that it takes as much hard work as it does being in love. Hard work is what helps you keep your marriage in good working order, as much as is possible when it comes to human relationships. By doing this workbook, you have also demonstrated an interest, understanding, and willingness to do that work.

My main goal in creating this program for couples before they walk down the aisle is to try to avoid walking straight into the 50% who end up divorced. And if you are already married, you hopefully have been able to use this to try to strengthen or repair your marriage.

Even though this has been work, hopefully some of it has been fun. Hopefully you both learned more about each other while doing this. Yet you also have probably learned a lot about yourselves as well.

Obviously, even the tasks in this workbook cannot completely prepare you for some of the curveballs life will throw you. Yet you already have an advantage over many other couples. Even couples who are a few years into a marriage may not have the insight you may have now from investing the time and effort into the work.

Let this also be a starting off point to work on any issues that may have come to light while working through these tasks. If you heard some alarm bells and saw some red flags, do not just blow that off. It does not mean one of you is "wrong" and the other one "right." It means you have identified some areas that could cause conflict, especially in times of crisis. Go ahead and move towards understanding those areas and working on them, either through your own exercises or even by speaking to someone as a couple about them.

You are now ready to continue on, whatever that looks like for your situation. It could be going ahead and getting that marriage license. It could be setting a date but a little further down the road than you originally intended. It could be doing more work first. Or it may even mean going your separate ways.

The bottom line is that there is no perfect key for success for love or for anything in life. The good news is that you have shown you care enough to work on your marriage before even walking down the aisle. And now I wish you the best of luck and the hope for you both to have your happily ever after.

About the Author

Affectionately known to his childhood friends as "Birdman," Dave Parrot born (January 31, 1958) on Long Island, New York, was the eldest of three sons born to William and Patricia. When told by his first grade teacher that he was "brain damaged," he found sports to be a great outlet for learning, growth, and character building for life. While at Wantagh High School, Dave was a three sport letterman in football, basketball, and lacrosse. The discipline of athletics taught him to believe that he could rise and prosper from any challenge he faced. At the age 17, his High School football career abruptly came to an end due to personal issues, and then, he experienced the break-up of his family due to divorce.

Dave learned early that "no wonderful and fulfilling life is without pain." Then, living in a world of anger and confusion, it was Dave's High School varsity basketball coach who gave him great words of encouragement. Coach Kalinowski said, "*Dave, you are a senior and we really need you to step up and become an important part of this team.*" Heart filled words at the right time were truly a gift from God. Dave did step up, and he experienced a thrilling season as the sixth man and true spark off the bench.

Inspirational lyrics that played big roles in Dave's comeback included; "You've got to get up every morning with a smile on your face and show the world all the love in your heart," by Carole King from her song "Beautiful," and the hit, "Feeling Stronger Every Day," from the band Chicago.

Dave quickly became a "student of life. He made a personal commitment to be an encourager (like Coach K) to anyone he meets on life's journey. One friend observes, "*Dave makes a great effort to listen, understand and remember, and he is always available to help. He is known to pose such questions to friends and acquaintances as, 'Why?' 'How can I help?' 'How can we improve?'*"

The majority of Dave's professional career has been spent in sales and company ownership. Dave says "Life is always a comeback." After varying degrees of business/life successes and failures, he often reverts to the fundamentals of discipline for new growth. "It is the failures that have taught me the most," he says.

Sadly in 2011, Dave faced his own divorce after almost 20 years of marriage which set him on a path of understanding relationships and marriage on a deeper level. His literary debut, 'Eyes Wide Open' (book and workbook) is the ultimate premarital book and he advises, "Any couple considering marriage should take the seminar, read the book and do the assignments in the workbook together. Too many people are getting married without really knowing each other. This is a recipe for failure. The exercises help couples get to know one another on a deeper level before making one of the biggest decisions of their lives."

Today, Dave makes his home in New Vernon, New Jersey is a happy man with three children, two sons and a daughter. Sam 21 is a fitness trainer, Jarred 19, has smartly opted for a gap year, to be part of a new business venture, rather than take on excessive college debt, and his youngster Gillian is in middle school playing three sports.

Dave has a BA in Communications from State University of New York at Oswego. He speaks, consults, and writes on a variety of life topics. Dave's other titles in a series are: "Stepping Up," "Single Fatherhood," and "Mounting a Life Comeback."

Contact Dave at 973-975-0927 or via email at dp@daveparrot.com to book a seminar or a couples coaching series

Made in the USA
San Bernardino, CA
12 June 2014